The Light Of Bethlehem Shines On

Sermons And Children's Messages For Advent And Christmas

Thomas A. Pilgrim

CSS Publishing Company, Inc., Lima, Ohio

THE LIGHT OF BETHLEHEM SHINES ON

Copyright © 2004 by
CSS Publishing Company, Inc.
Lima, Ohio

Scripture quotations are from the *New Revised Standard Version of the Bible*, copyright 1989 by the Division of Christian Education of the National Council of the Churches of Christ in the USA. Used by permission.

Library of Congress Cataloging-in-Publication Data pending

For more information about CSS Publishing Company resources, visit our website at www.csspub.com or e-mail us at custserv@csspub.com or call (800) 241-4056.

ISBN 0-7880-2334-9   PRINTED IN U.S.A.

This is for Shirley
who still shares with me
the light which shines on her

Table Of Contents

First Sunday After Christmas

Epiphany Of Our Lord

Preface

I have traveled to the Holy Land eight times. One of the highlights of those journeys was visiting Bethlehem. It is a meaningful and thrilling experience to go there, and it never loses its mystery and wonder.

I have been to the shepherds' fields and tried to imagine what that must have been like, being out there on some dark night.

I have been to a gift shop where one of the owners comes out to the bus and prays the Lord's Prayer in Aramaic, and I have tried to listen with a new hearing.

I have bent down low to enter the short door of the old church, knowing this is a sign of humility, and remembering also it was a way to keep out enemies on horseback in olden times.

I have stood in that sanctuary, which is 1,600 years old and thought how in the fullness of time God fulfilled the dreams of prophets and the longings of a young couple.

I have gone down the steps to that old stable, which was transformed into the holy place, and I have knelt down and kissed the star.

I have risen with a heartwarming thought; joy to the world, the Lord is come.

I have not been there lately though, because there has been so much trouble and suffering in those holy places. Even the church has been the site, not of consolation, but of conflict.

In spite of that, the light of Bethlehem still shines on us. It is a light no darkness can put out. I hope to return to that place in the not-too-distant future. Until then, I will simply remember a little town, a quiet place, a holy night, an infant king, the light of a star, and the light which still shines on us.

Thomas A. Pilgrim

In The Darkness Of Despair, There Is The Light Of Hope

A student at The University of Georgia got a job as a disc jockey at a little radio station in Commerce, Georgia. He also got a room at a hotel in town and commuted to school, which was not far away. Sometimes at night, he would crawl out of his window and sit on the roof of the hotel. He would look out over that little town. One night when he was up there, he wrote a song called "City Lights." The rest is country music history. His name was Bill Anderson.

An Episcopalian minister in Boston worked himself to near exhaustion. He was on the verge of a complete breakdown. He was greatly depressed and almost gave up in despair. But, he took some time off and went away on a trip. He traveled to a place where he had never been before. He saw the lights of a small town, walked along its streets, and in those lights he found hope again. He wrote a song which has in it these words:

> O little town of Bethlehem, how still we see thee lie;
> above thy deep and dreamless sleep the silent stars go by.
> Yet in thy dark streets shineth the everlasting light;
> the hopes and fears of all the years are met in thee
> tonight.[1]

The rest is church history. His name was Phillips Brooks.

I have seen the lights of Bethlehem. Those lights of Bethlehem are everlasting lights. Across 2,000 years there has never been a time when those lights have gone out. The lights of Bethlehem still shine. The light of Bethlehem still shines on us.

On these Sundays, in the Advent season, and beyond, I want to share with you how the light of Bethlehem still shines on us.

9

The scripture lesson for today comes from the book of Isaiah. It was written during a dark and dangerous time. During a period of 150 years, both the northern and southern kingdoms were threatened by their enemies. Both kingdoms fell and the people suffered the worst kind of defeat and agony. Eventually, even Jerusalem was overrun, the walls torn down, and the temple destroyed, but in the midst of those years of darkness, even before the worst had come, the people were offered hope. A singer, a preacher, gave them words of hope. Here are the words he gave them:

> *The people who walked in darkness have seen a great light; those who dwelt in a land of deep darkness, on them has light shined.*

The rest is Bible history. His name was Isaiah.

The people who heard those words of God from that preacher needed to hear them because there was darkness all around them. Powerful enemies had been trying to destroy them for centuries, and they were on the verge of destruction, but in the darkness of despair, words of hope came to them.

The people living during that time, and on up to the time of Jesus, believed good and evil were equated with light and darkness. They believed in the powers of darkness and the powers of light.

We do not think that way in the modern world, and yet, we still use such phrases as, "It's a dark time," "The dark night of the soul," "The dark side," "I'm wandering around in the dark," "There's a light at the end of the tunnel," and "I'm beginning to see the light."

We use these words and phrases because they describe what many of us experience. These common feelings have always been a part of the human experience. There have been many times in history when it has been so.

Our world today has a good bit of darkness in it, in spite of the light which is available.

Sometimes, often, this happens on a personal level. That is how we see this truth in our lives today. Many people feel hopeless. Many people experience despair.

Even in this season of the year, which should bring out the best in us, sometimes the worst comes out.

One writer imagined a conversation between Archie Bunker and his son-in-law Meathead, who asked Archie if he knew what Advent meant. Archie said, "Yeah, you add up all your hostile feelings and then you vent them on somebody. It's people like you that make me enjoy Advent."[2]

The darkness of despair can be a common experience even in this season of the year. But the season of Advent we begin today has a message for us, and for all who experience the darkness of despair, there is a light of hope. The lights of Bethlehem still shine on us.

Think about this today by starting out with this fact:

I

The light of hope still shines on you.

The light of hope shines brightest in despair. Listen to what Isaiah wrote, "The people who walked in darkness have seen a great light." This was their hope for the present and for the future.

It really does not take much light to shine in the darkness. A little light goes a long way.

When I was in the Army, we went for night training. We stood on a little hill there in the darkness. We looked far down into the valley. Suddenly, a person out there struck a match. We could see clearly that little light shining far away in the darkness.

A woman was talking with her doctor about her husband. She said, "My husband thinks he's a refrigerator." The doctor said, "Well, you know, that is really harmless." She answered, "I know, but he sleeps with his mouth open, and the light keeps me awake."

A little light goes a long way.

There is a light that still shines upon us. It is the light of hope.

Do you know what that light of hope is? Isaiah called it a "great light." But it was not that great in the beginning. Very few people even noticed it at first.

Isaiah tells us what it is: "For to us a child is born, to us a son is given." The light would shine in the face of a child.

United Methodist theologian, and preacher, Paul Scherer, said we can have hope in a world "where Christmas comes out of a stable, the Son of God out of a smelly, little village, and twenty centuries of Christianity out of a tomb."[3]

He is the light that shines in the darkness. He is the light of hope — the source of hope — the reason for hope.

Some will miss it, of course. I walked around at one of the malls the other night. It was the busiest shopping day of the year. I saw a lot of people working really hard, frantically trying to purchase some happiness, hoping to bring some light into the darkness of their lives and the lives of those they love. But, the real light of hope is such a small thing it can almost be missed.

A man took his granddaughter to see the live manger scene at their church. She stood there looking at everything — the manger, the holy family, the Wise Men, and the shepherds. Then she pointed to the star. He asked her if she thought the light shone into the stable. She said, "Of course it does. That's why it's so bright inside. But, granddaddy, you can't see how the light shines in, unless you get down and look up."[4]

Put yourself in a place where you can see the real light of hope. It will shine on you. Then this:

II

The light of hope will enable you to find your way.

This light of hope will shine on the road you travel.

Isaiah wrote, "Those who dwelt in a land of deep darkness, on them has light shined." Not only had they seen a great light, that light had shone on them.

Because of the light of hope which has shone on us, we will be able to find our way.

There was a little boy whose name was Leslie Hope. At school, the teacher called the roll last name first. So, it was Hope, Leslie. The other children started calling him, "Hopeless." He did not like that, because he was not hopeless. He was a happy person. Later, he changed his name to Bob.[5]

Whatever is facing you, and whatever darkness surrounds you, there is a light that shines in the darkness, and that light shines on you.

That light will enable you to find your way.

Virginia Law told of her experience as a missionary in the Congo. She said that at their mission station, there were men who served as night sentries. They carried oil lanterns. One night, one of them brought her a message. She noticed his lantern and said, "That lamp doesn't give much light, does it?" He replied, "No. It doesn't. But, it shines as far as I can step."[6]

You can find your way, as far as you can step, to wherever you need to go, in the light of hope which shines on you. Then, one more thing:

III

The light of hope can be shared by you.

Not only can you find your way, you can share this light so that others can find the way.

Isaiah also wrote how the joy of the nation had increased, how the people rejoiced, how the yoke of their burden was broken — for this child shall be called "Wonderful Counselor, Mighty God, Everlasting Father, Prince of Peace."

You can share the light of hope, and increase joy, and break yokes of despair.

You can be a witness of this light by living the meaning of it, by being a person of hope, by reflecting the light of Christ, by sharing the warmth of it in your daily life, by inviting other people to come into this lighthouse to learn of the light and feel the warmth of it. In this light, they will find hope.

Centuries ago, a nobleman in Europe built a church for his people. It was a place of beauty. He thought of everything. But when it opened, and a great crowd of people came there, some of them noticed there were no lamps. The nobleman pointed to lamp holders all down both sides. Then, he gave each family a lamp and said, "Each time you are here, the place where you sit will be lighted." It was up to them to bring the light and share it.[7]

One year, the youth of the church we were serving decided to have a live manger scene in front of the church. One of the men built a stable. The Sunday afternoon of the first performance, I went to the church to put the light in the stable. I carefully held it

13

in place and secured it with several nails. I bent down to pick up one more nail, and when I looked back up, the light fell and hit me right above my left eye. I ran inside and called my wife and told her to come quickly and take me to the emergency clinic. I was bleeding too badly to see how to drive. When she asked what happened, I told her, "The star of Bethlehem fell on me." But, that night, people came by to see a baby warmed by the light of a star.

I wonder, in this Advent season, if you would be willing to let the light of Bethlehem fall on you? And would you then be willing to be a person who shares the light?

---

1. Phillips Brooks, "O Little Town Of Bethlehem," *The United Methodist Hymnal* (Nashville: The United Methodist Publishing House, 1989), p. 20.

2. William J. Carl, III, *Waiting For The Lord* (Nashville: Abingdon Press, 1988), p. 16.

3. Paul Scherer, *Love Is A Spendthrift* (New York: Harper & Brothers, 1961), p. 98.

4. Lamar J. Brooks, "... And On Earth, Peace," *Award Winning Sermons* (Nashville: Broadman Press, 1979), p. 33.

5. Ernest A. Fitzgerald, *You Can Believe* (Nashville-New York: Abingdon Press, 1975), p. 68.

6. James W. Moore, *Attitude Is Your Paintbrush* (Nashville: Dimension For Living, 1998), p. 37.

7. James W. Moore, *Some Things Are Too Good Not To Be True* (Nashville: Dimension For Living, 1994), p. 117.

Lighting Of The First Advent Candle

Scripture Reading — Isaiah 40:1-5

> *Comfort, O comfort my people, says your God. Speak tenderly to Jerusalem, and cry to her that she has served her term, that her penalty is paid, that she has received from the Lord's hand double for all her sins. A voice cries out: "In the wilderness prepare the way of the Lord, make straight in the desert a highway for our God. Every valley shall be lifted up, and every mountain and hill be made low; the uneven ground shall become level, and the rough places a plain. Then the glory of the Lord shall be revealed, and all people shall see it together, for the mouth of the Lord has spoken."*

Leader: This candle we light today helps us to remember that Jesus Christ is the light of the world, and in him we find hope.

People: Let this light of hope shine on us. Thanks be to God.

Prayer

O God, at the beginning of this Advent season, prepare us to receive the good news of the coming of the Lord. Let us each prepare the way of the Lord into our lives. Help us to look for him, and to receive him. Let us pause for a moment to slow down and open our lives to the possibility of something new beginning in us.

We come together to worship thee and to sing praises to thy name, for thou art the only God, and thy deeds are many and great. Thou art our creator, and we are thy children, the sheep of thy pasture. We thank thee for thy abundant goodness toward us.

We seek thy help, O God, for the times in which we live have many possibilities for darkness and despair, and yet in thy Son, Jesus Christ, there is a light that overcomes the darkness which is all around us. He is that light, the light of the world. Shine that light upon us, in us, and through us, that all the world may see the light and be drawn to it, and then find in it goodness, warmth, comfort, salvation, and hope.

Forgive our sins, which are many. Lift our hope, which sometimes falters. Strengthen our faith, which sometimes gives way. Renew our strength, which sometimes fails. Broaden our vision, which is sometimes narrow. Perfect our love, which is sometimes faulty.

Bless those in our church family and community who suffer from great illnesses, whether of the body, mind, or spirit. Bless thy world, O God, for all the world needs the touch of thy healing hands. Bless the work of this church, and the work of thy church throughout all the earth. Bless the leaders of the world and all the great people of the world. In this season may we know peace on earth, and good will among those with whom thou art pleased.

We make this our prayer in the name of thy Son, Jesus Christ, who is our Savior and Lord. Amen.

The People Of The Light, #1

Object: a Chrismon tree and a scroll Chrismon

Boys and girls, I am so glad you are here today. Here we are on the first Sunday in Advent. Notice that the color for this new season is blue. Sometimes we use purple, but we are using blue. What I would like for us to do is talk about those people who were a part of the first Christmas, and I want us to call them the people of the light. These are people who were involved in the first Christmas in some way, or who were touched by it.

Today, we begin with Isaiah the prophet, who lived a long time before Jesus was born. Even though he did not ever see Jesus, because he lived so long before his birth, he did know about Jesus. Isaiah was a prophet for God. A prophet was a person who spoke for God.

Each Sunday we are going to look at some of the symbols we have on our Chrismon tree. These are called Chrismons. They are Christ symbols. They remind us of Jesus Christ. This one today is a scroll, and it helps us to think about how the prophets of old wrote about the coming of Jesus into the world. They did not have books like we do today, so they would write on a large piece of paper or maybe a skin of some kind, and then roll it up like this one. They were much bigger than this is, but this helps us get the idea.

Isaiah, more than any of the other prophets, told about the coming of Jesus into the world. His people, who lived in Jerusalem, were in big trouble. They were surrounded by mean and dangerous enemies. They wanted God to come and save them, to send a Savior to help them. They looked for a new, mighty, and powerful king. But God had a better idea. He would send them a Savior who would save not just them, but the whole world. He would be

17

a new king, all right, but a different kind of king, and his kingdom would not be just a worldly kingdom. It would be a kingdom that would live in the hearts of all people. It would be the rule of God in the lives of people.

So, Isaiah the prophet was one of the people of the light, because he saw that light of Jesus shining long before it ever did. And he told the people God would send the light.

You can be a person of the light also. You can let the light of Jesus shine on you.

Second Sunday In Advent
John 1:1-13

In The Darkness Of Suffering, There Is The Light Of Life

Several years ago, I read Sidney Sheldon's Novel, *The Windmills Of The Gods*. I read it with a good deal of interest, though it was not about windmills and it was not about God. I was struck by a scene where the heroine had lost her young husband, a doctor. She was left with her two children, and was trying to put her life back together. She laid awake one night thinking how easy it would be to die, how happiness and love were so easily snatched away. Then this thought ran through her mind, "The world is Dachau, and we are all Jews."[1]

Such is the darkness of suffering so many of us go through. If we have not gone through suffering in the past, we will face some kind of suffering in the future. Perhaps some of us are facing it in the present.

Add to that another story:

It was the Christmas of 1968. Gerald Coffee was spending his third Christmas in prison. His Vietnamese guards gave some candy to him and to his fellow prisoners-of-war. He heard the guards outside talking and laughing with their families, celebrating Christmas. One of the guards had a son who was about three or four. Coffee thought of his own children back home. He ate the candy and looked at the red and silver foil. He began to form that foil into three shapes — a swan, a rosette, and a star. He thought of the star of Bethlehem. He placed those three shapes above his bed. He laid there looking at them. Then, he began thinking about the birth of Christ. He knew it was only faith that was getting him through this experience. He wrote later that in that place there was nothing to distract him from the awesomeness of Christmas, even though he had lost everything that defined who he was. He wrote, "Yet, I continued to find strength within. I realized that although I was

19

hurting and lonely and scared, this might be the most significant Christmas of my life."[2]

These are two stories of human suffering. In the darkness of suffering, one person saw nothing but the darkness. The other saw the light.

On these Sundays in Advent, we are thinking about the theme: The light of Bethlehem still shines on. Today, I want to center our thinking around this: In the darkness of suffering, there is the light of life. That is a light which still shines on us.

Our scripture lesson for today is not about the birth of Jesus, or about Mary getting the news, or Joseph getting the news. It is, instead, about the very beginning of the news, "In the beginning was the word, and the word was with God, and the word was God."

The first eighteen verses of John's Gospel are called his prologue. It is the long statement about the word becoming flesh. The word is *logos*, the creative power of God at work in the universe, God *himself.*

The Bible begins with this same kind of language, "In the beginning God created the heavens and the earth." And the next thing God created was the light, "Let there be light."

This creative power in the universe, this word, this *logos*, God *himself*, has come into the world in human form. For Saint John tells us, "In him was life, and the life was the light of men."

Saint John also tells us that at a certain point God *himself* stepped onto the stage of human history, and when he did that, he stepped right into the middle of human suffering.

The Jews were suffering under the rule of Rome. It is true that the Romans had brought about a time of peace, but it was because no one could oppose them. They had advanced human life in many ways, and yet the thumb of Rome had come down hard upon everyone.

Add to that the lives those people had to face filled with disease and hunger, sickness and death, injustice and persecution. Yet, in the midst of all that suffering, the life of Jesus was, "the light of all people."

I want to say to you that whatever it is you face, Christmas holds for you the promise of help and hope, the promise of light and love, the promise of joy and peace. In the darkness of your own suffering, there is a light that still shines. It is the light of Christmas, and for you, Jesus Christ is the light of life.

Because the light of Bethlehem still shines on, let us think about what this means for us today. Think first of this:

I

Jesus Christ is the light which will overcome any darkness.

That is the testimony of Saint John in his Gospel, "The light shines in the darkness, and the darkness has not overcome it."

Saint John is giving us the conclusion of the story he is writing at the beginning. He is telling us ahead of time how it turns out. Jesus had already defeated the worst kind of darkness — the darkness of death. God's answer to death was resurrection.

Before I read the book, *The Horse Whisperer*, I saw the movie. I went into a bookstore and read the last few pages to see if the book ended the same way the movie did. It did not. Then, I bought the book and read it.

Saint John is saving us the trouble of flipping over to the end. He is telling us right at the beginning that this is how it turns out: "The light shines in the darkness, and the darkness has not overcome it." That is the only reason this book was written.

Do you know what this means for us? It means that no matter what we face he has already defeated it — already conquered it — already overcome it.

This means the great good news of Christmas is also the great good news of Easter and resurrection and of victory. Jesus Christ has already won the victory, and everything you and I could ever possibly face has already been defeated.

That is why we bow down around a manger. It is not because Jesus is a sweet, cute, bouncing, baby boy. It is because of what he became and what he did. He drove the darkness right out of our lives.

A little boy was telling his parents about being in Sunday school. He said, "My teacher is the grandmother of Jesus." They said, "Oh, no. You just have it mixed up. She's not really the grandmother of

Jesus." He replied, "I know she is. She showed us his picture and just bragged on him."

This is something to brag about — what God has done with his Son.

I hope you will remember this.

United Methodist Bishop Ernest Fitzgerald told about a man who taught Sunday school class at a little church in the Great Smoky Mountains of North Carolina. One Sunday, his lesson was about, "What I Have Learned Thus Far." One of the things he mentioned was this, "Never forget in the dark what God has told you in the light."[3]

I hope you remember that Jesus Christ is the light which will overcome any darkness.

Think next of this:

II

Jesus Christ is the light which will enlighten your life.

Saint John also tells us this, "The true light that enlightens every man was coming into the world."

During his ministry, Jesus brought people from the darkness out into the light. He called Legion out of a cemetery. He called Lazarus out of a tomb. He called Zacchaeus out of the shade. He called Bartimaeus out of blindness. At one point, Jesus announced boldly, "I am the light of the world. Whoever follows me will never walk in darkness but will have the light of life."

I love the story of the little boy in the Christmas play at church. He played the part of Jesus as a grown man in a glimpse into the future. The boy had one line he was to speak, "I am the light of the world." But when his great moment came, he forgot the words. He could not think of them. His mother was seated right in the front row. She could stand it no longer, so she fed him the line, "I am the light of the world." The boy saw her, smiled, took a deep breath, and said, "My mother is the light of the world."

Jesus is the light of life — the light of the world — the true light that enlightens everyone. Since he enlightens everyone that means he will enlighten your life.

The light which he is, will reach into the dark corners of your existence, and shed light upon all of life's perplexities. The light which he is, will warm your heart and, in this season, fill your living with love and good will. The light which he is, will shine across the road you travel and enable you to find your way.

A family visited Carlsbad Caverns while on vacation. They were down in the caves with a large group of tourists. The guide wanted to show them how dark it really was. He had the lights turned off. The daughter of this family grabbed her big brother's hand. The brother said to her, "Don't worry. There is someone here who knows how to turn on the lights."[4]

Remember that Jesus Christ will enlighten your life. He knows how to turn on the lights. He is the light.

Finally, think about this:

III

Jesus Christ is the light which will empower your living.

That is the final thing I want us to hear from Saint John. He wrote, "To all who received him, who believed in his name, he gave power to become children of God."

It is interesting to me that at our home we receive our electricity not from the Georgia Electric Company, or Georgia Light Company, but from Georgia Power Company. The light comes from the power.

For Christians, it is the other way around; the power comes from the light.

Jesus Christ is the light which will empower you. He will empower your living. This is a special kind of living. It is not just power to get through the day. Look again at what Saint John has written. It is power "to become children of God."

That is who we are. That is who God has called us to be. That is what Jesus Christ empowers us to become: the children of God.

I saw a little part of a Christmas television special where a young female singer on the show was all dressed up for Christmas. She wore a red dress. Her hair was blond and green and pink. After her song, she was interviewed briefly. She said Christmas was her favorite holiday. I thought maybe there was more there than I imagined. Then she said, "Christmas is for children." I knew then she did not understand it. Like so many people, she had missed the significance of Christmas. It is not a holiday for children. It is the celebration of a great cosmic event in which God came boldly into the midst of human history to take back his creation and make his creatures become the children of God.

That is what Saint Paul was getting at when he wrote to the Christians in Rome, that all who are led by the spirit of God are children of God, and if they are the children of God, then they are the heirs of God and joint heirs with Christ. That is, if we are willing to suffer with him and thereby be glorified with him.

That sheds a new light on the darkness of human suffering.

Do you really want your living to be empowered? Do you really want Jesus Christ, who is the light, to bring you to the light that shines, in the midst of your suffering? It just might cause you to do something you never would have thought of before. You just might find yourself being a light person, working for the power company, spreading the light, sharing the light, giving away the light in the darkness of suffering.

That is part of what it means to become a child of God.

A wealthy man enjoyed taking his son on business trips. Often on these trips, the man would purchase priceless works of art. He filled his home with these paintings. The boy grew to manhood and when war broke out, he went to serve his country. In just a few months, the man received word his son had died in battle, trying to save the lives of some of his friends. When the next Christmas came, the man found it difficult to get through the season. The suffering he had experienced was too much. But on Christmas morning, a young soldier came to his door and presented him with a portrait of his son. The young soldier was among those whose lives had been saved. The father placed the portrait over his fireplace. He would often sit in front of it and think of his son. Several years later, the man died. His lawyer carried out his will. The instructions were that the home and everything in it was to be sold at auction. The first thing to be sold was the portrait of the man's son. When the auctioneer called out, "What am I bid?" no one seemed to want the portrait. To move things along, a man in the

24

back said, "Ten dollars." The auctioneer said, "Going, going, gone. Sold for ten dollars. The auction is over." There was an outcry as people exclaimed, "What! What do you mean?" The auctioneer explained, "The terms of the will are very clear: Whoever chooses the son, receives everything."[5]

Saint Paul also told the Roman Christians, "He who did not spare his son, but gave him up for all of us, will he not also give us all things with him?"

If you will choose the Son, you will have it all, for you will have the light of life, the one who said, "I have come that you might have life and that more abundantly."

---

1. Sidney Sheldon, *The Windmills Of The Gods* (New York: William Morrow and Company, Inc., 1987), p. 120.

2. John Killinger, "Entertaining The Mystery," *Pulpit Digest*, November-December, 1992 (San Francisco: Harper, 1992), p. 16.

3. Ernest A. Fitzgerald, *Keeping Pace* (Greensboro, North Carolina: Pace Communications, Inc., 1988), p. 99.

4. Brian Kelley Bauknight, *Gracious Imperatives* (Nashville: Abingdon Press, 1992), p. 39.

5. Source unknown, a story off the Internet.

Lighting Of The Second Advent Candle

Scripture Reading — Isaiah 61:1-4

The spirit of the Lord God is upon me, because the Lord has anointed me; he has sent me to bring good news to the oppressed, to bind up the brokenhearted, to proclaim liberty to the captives, and release to the prisoners; to proclaim the year of the Lord's favor, and the day of vengeance of our God; to comfort all who mourn; to provide for those who mourn in Zion — to give them a garland instead of ashes, the oil of gladness instead of mourning, the mangle of praise instead of a faint spirit. They will be called oaks of righteousness, the planting of the Lord, to display his glory. They shall build up the ancient ruins, they shall raise up the former devastations; they shall repair the ruined cities, the devastations of many generations.

Leader: This candle we light today helps us to remember that Jesus Christ is the light of the world, and in him we find life.

People: **Let this light of life shine on us. Thanks be to God.**

Prayer

O God, our Heavenly Father, as we gather today we seek to praise thee and to worship thee, for thou art our creator, sustainer, savior, and friend. Lift our hearts in this Advent season and open them widely, that the King of glory may come in. May we be ready for his coming so that he would find a place to live in us. Fill us with anticipation and expectancy.

We thank thee, gracious God, for all thy blessings upon us, and we thank thee for the gift of life. Father, thou hast blessed each of us far beyond anything we would be able to deserve. For family, friends, faith, work, and all of life's joys, for all of life's great moments, we thank thee, O God. We thank thee for thy Son and our Savior, for in him is light, and the light is the life of us all. In him there is no darkness at all. Fill us with the light, and shine thy light on all the paths we follow. May we always follow after thee.

Lead us, O God, into new adventures with thee. Enable us to learn thy ways, as we see them lived out and taught in the life of our Lord, Jesus, who is the Christ. Make us students of his ways. Lead us into new avenues of service, as we seek to follow his example. Lead us to worship thee and to reach new depths in our devotion as we surrender our lives to thee.

Strengthen this, thy church, O God. May we be stalwart witnesses for thee and thy kingdom. Lead us to find new and better ways to serve thee. Make us faithful, generous, compassionate, forward looking, and vigilant.

Forgive us when we are wrong. Make us humble when we are right. Make us kind in the face of opposition. Make us optimistic in the face of doubt. Make us progressive in the face of inertia.

Bless the sick, lonely, troubled, and fearful of our church family and community. Be with all who mourn, and may we be with them. Touch the lives of hurting people the world over. Touch them through us and our ministries of help, hope, and healing. We ask in it the name of the one who is to come to bring life, Jesus Christ, our Lord and Savior. Amen.

The People Of The Light, #2

Object: a candle Chrismon for the Chrismon tree

Good morning boys and girls. I am so glad to see all of you here today. This is the second Sunday in the season of Advent, and we are a little bit closer to Christmas. On these Sundays we are talking together about the people of the light. These are people who are somehow involved in Christmas, or who are touched by it.

Today, I want us to think about John. John was not there when Jesus was born, because he was born several years after Jesus was born. But this John is the man who wrote the Gospel of John, and our scripture lesson for today is from the book he wrote. He was, of course, touched by the coming of Jesus because he became a follower of Jesus, a disciple. He, and his brother, James, had been fishermen, along with Peter and Andrew. But Jesus asked them all to follow him.

Much later, after Jesus had died, was resurrected, and went back to heaven to be with God, his disciples began to write down what they had known of him, the things they saw him do and heard him say. One of these was John. In his book, he tells all about Jesus.

He begins that book by telling us that Jesus was like a light that shines in the darkness. Look at this Chrismon from our tree. It is a candle. We have it on our tree to remind that Jesus is the light that shines in the darkness.

John tells us something that is very important about Jesus. He says that this light we find in Jesus is the light of life. That means he helps us to live, and we find our lives in him, we live best when we live with him. He is the light that helps us find our way through the darkness.

Jesus said one time, "I am the light of the world." People in those days were afraid of the dark. He was the light for them, and he is the light for us as well.

If you live with Jesus Christ in your life, you will never be alone in the dark.

Third Sunday In Advent
Luke 2:1-5

In The Darkness Of Oppression, There Is The Light Of Salvation

I was staying at a hotel in a small town, near a large city. My room was upstairs on the front, overlooking the street. The noise from below finally died down, but I still was unable to sleep for a long time. Late in the night, I was startled by a man pounding on the door downstairs. I heard voices, and I could tell the manager was talking with this man about needing a room. As I listened closer, I learned that it was a man and his wife. They had come a long way. The young wife was expecting a child any moment. They needed a place to stay.

The manager of the hotel explained to them how all the rooms had already been taken. There was an unusual amount of tourists for that time of the year. Many of them were on business, in town for the same reason I was. There simply was no place for the couple. But, I remember him saying, "I'll tell you what I can do. There's a place down in the basement, where we keep the animals. I'm sorry, that's all I have. But this time of the year, it's really the warmest place I have, being below ground."

I listened intently and heard steps as they went around the corner of the building. I lay awake a long time, knowing a little baby could be born here, and early in the wee hours I fought sleep, wondering if I might be able to hear a baby's cry.

Here on the third Sunday In Advent, we are getting closer to the celebration of the Savior's birth. We are in that time of anticipation — expectancy — looking forward. That is the feeling in the air on this Sunday in Advent.

There was a custom in the far north, where the nights are six months long. After spending long months in the darkness, the people gather out on a hillside to celebrate the return of the sunlight. They would sing, "The sun is coming to us again."

31

Here in this time of anticipation, we seem to hear the words of the prophet Isaiah echoing down through the centuries, "The people who walked in darkness have seen a great light."

It was certainly a time of anticipation for Joseph and Mary as they left their home in Nazareth and made their way down into Judea, to the town of Bethlehem, Joseph's ancestral home.

Late in the evening, they came through Jerusalem, and took that little road which led out to Bethlehem. As they came near Bethlehem, they saw only a few lights still on. They heard a few voices in the night, and someone's old dog was barking in the distance.

They went to the Bethlehem Inn, for it had been a long journey and they were weary. They were glad to take that space where the animals were kept. There was a room in the inn, but it was down in the basement in an area carved out of the side of a sandstone hill. It was probably the warmest place in town, also, but none of that really mattered to them. There was something that caused them to forget their weariness and overlook the uncomfortable surroundings, for they were thrilled in their hearts with the anticipated birth of their child.

This child would be the Savior of the world. The people walking in darkness would receive a great light. It would be the light of salvation.

On these Sundays, we are thinking about the theme: The light of Bethlehem still shines on us. Today, our thoughts turn to this: In the darkness of oppression, there is the light of salvation.

Joseph and Mary went to Bethlehem for one reason. All of these people were living under the oppression of Rome. It had been that way for centuries. First, the surrounding enemies had conquered Israel, then Judah, then came the deportation to Babylon. That was followed by a time of freedom. Soon the Greeks came, and then the Romans. The people were oppressed. They needed a Savior and they knew it. The irony is, the Savior came, and yet many did not even know it.

The salvation he brought would be greater than any political freedom. It would be broader than the borders of any kingdom or empire.

The light he brought into the world, the light of salvation, still shines. It shines into the darkness of any, and every, kind of oppression.

Perhaps some of us are oppressed today by fear, sin, sorrow, failure, or suffering of some kind. Christmas brings to all of us the good news of the Savior's birth. In the darkness of oppression, the light of salvation still shines.

Let me suggest some things for us which enable us to receive the Savior and stand in the light of salvation:

I

Look for him expectantly.

That is something basic. Look for him expectantly.

If we do not do this, we will not find him. We will not see him. We will not know of his coming to us if we are not looking for him.

We always look forward to the birth of a baby expectantly. That is why we use the term "expecting." To keep from using the word "pregnant" we sometimes use a more proper-sounding word, like "expecting," or we say, "in a family way." That says nothing about the reality of the situation, the reality is that a baby is on its way into the world.

Mary was pregnant, and she and Joseph were expecting that little fellow to arrive immediately. They went to Bethlehem knowing he could be born at any time. That ride on the donkey must have encouraged him along.

All of the people involved in the first Christmas had this same sense of expectancy. Not only these parents, but the shepherds and the Wise Men as well. They all came to Bethlehem expecting to find him.

That is what we need, this sense of expectancy.

So many of us in the modern world have such a low sense of expectancy. We have no expectations. We feel we have already seen it all. We spend our lives aiming at nothing and hitting it. We are not looking for anything, not expecting anything.

My wife grew up in the low country of South Carolina, across the river from Savannah, Georgia. Once, when we were there visiting her mother, I was reading a local paper. I saw an ad that said, "Wanted, a good woman who will clean, sew, cook, fish, dig worms, and owns a good boat and motor. Please send picture of boat and motor." Nothing has ever happened to the man who placed that ad and nothing ever will.

What we must do is work on our sense of expectancy.

An ambitious young man asked an experienced salesman to share with him how he had been so successful. The older salesman said, "There is no great secret to it. You just have to jump at every opportunity that comes along." The young man wanted to know how you could tell when an opportunity was coming along. The older man said, "You can't tell. You just have to keep on jumping."

In all areas of our lives, we must expect something to happen. This is especially true of Christmas and what it can mean to us. We can only get out of it what we are expecting.

There is a novel that places Jesus in the modern world. The name of it is *Joshua*. That is the name of Jesus in this story, and the other books in this series. At one point, Joshua explained to a man how we see what we are looking at differently. Joshua earned his living working with wood. He told the man we look at life with different vision. We see what we want to see. Three men may look at the same tree. One sees valuable lumber. Another sees firewood. The third sees a work of art.[1]

That is the way Christmas is. We must cultivate within ourselves the sense of expectancy about the Savior being born anew in us.

Let me remind you of something else:

II

Prepare for him thoroughly.

That is something else which is basic. Prepare for him thoroughly. We will miss him if we do not do this. We have to make the necessary preparations just as we have to prepare for a baby.

Mary and Joseph made the best preparations they could for the birth of this child. They were traveling all the way from Nazareth to Bethlehem. Sometimes you just have to do the best you can with what you have, where you are. Mary and Joseph did that.

If we do not prepare thoroughly for Christmas, it will pass us by and we will be none the better for it.

Maybe the question we face is not, "How would you like to experience Christmas?" but "How would you like to completely miss Christmas this year?" How would you like to not be affected by Christmas at all this year?

That is a danger so many of us face: that we will leave some important things undone.

Some years ago, Dr. John Brokhoff reminded us, in an Advent sermon, of a game we all played as a child. One person hides his or her eyes, while the others go hide themselves. Then, after counting to a certain number, the person who is "it," says, "Ready or not — here I come!"[2]

That is the way it is with Christmas and the birth of the Savior. Ready or not, Christmas comes, but if you want his light to shine on you, you must get ready.

Prepare for his coming. Open your heart and mind to this great truth about Christ being born — God's only Son coming into the world — becoming God with us — getting down to our eye level — taking upon himself the human experience — identifying himself with us and all we suffer through — enduring all our sins, sorrows, hurts, and shame, even death — and then winning a victory over all of this for us because he is the Savior. Remember all these basic things about his birth, and then open your heart and mind to this Savior being born in you.

There is an old story about a slave woman who had a great Christian faith. She could not read, but the children she cared for had taught her to recognize the name of Jesus. She knew it when she saw it. Every evening she would sit down with the Bible and run her fingers up and down the pages searching for the name of Jesus.

In the same spirit, let us be preparing ourselves thoroughly for his coming.

Let me remind you of something else:

III

Welcome him graciously.

That is the other very basic thing to remember. Welcome him graciously.

We will never know he has come if we do not do this. We must open our lives to him.

We must always do this for a baby. A baby will always change your life.

Mary and Joseph opened their lives to this baby. They received him as a precious gift.

We know everyone did not receive him that way. Most folks in Bethlehem never even knew what had happened. Old, mean Herod was not at all happy about it; he had a very hard time with the birth of Jesus. But most people just missed it entirely.

You need to receive him in a gracious way.

I was out one afternoon trying to find the home of one of our church members. I knew I was in the right neighborhood, but I could not find the house. I knocked on a door, hoping to find some- one who could tell me where to go. An older man opened the door and before I could introduce myself to him, and let him know that I was from the United Methodist church, he said, "Hi! Come in!" It was a gracious welcome to a stranger.

Would you give that kind of welcome to the Savior? Would you welcome him graciously?

A number of years ago, on Christmas Eve, the Altanta airport was iced in. Anxious passengers were hoping to catch their flights home. For a while, all flights were cancelled. But, things began to open up. Passengers listened for their flights and rushed to board them. A couple of people spotted one man in a fine business suit who seemed unconcerned, going about his work, reading reports, his first-class seat, probably, confirmed. They thought he was an- other Ebenezer Scrooge. When a young soldier appeared with a low-priority ticket, hoping to get a seat on the flight to New Or- leans, he was told there was little hope. He was almost frantic. He was going to Vietnam in less than a month and he said this might be his last Christmas at home. The agent was sorry, but there was nothing he could do. When the boarding began, the seats were called out and the plane began filling up. The businessman in the expensive suit walked up to the agent and said, "I have a confirmed ticket. I'd like to give my seat to this young man." The tears ran down the soldier's face as the man told him, "Good luck. Have a fine Christmas. Good luck." As the plane pulled away, there was a glow in the hearts of all who had seen what had taken place.[3]

What if this Christmas you and I could open up a place for the Savior? What kind of glow might burn in us if we could open our lives to the light of the Savior's birth? Won't you give him a place? Welcome him graciously into the place where you live.

---

1. Joseph F. Girzone, *Joshua* (New York: Macmillan Publishing Company, 1983), p. 67.

2. John R. Brokhoff, *Wrinkled Wrappings* (Lima, Ohio: CSS Publishing Company, Inc., 1975), p. 13.

3. Ray Jenkins, "Drama At Gate 67," *The Gift Of Christmas* (Norwalk, Connecticut: The C. R. Gibson Company, 1987), p. 55.

Lighting Of The Third Advent Candle

Scripture Reading — Micah 5:2-5

But you, O Bethlehem of Ephrathah, who are one of the little clans of Judah, from you shall come forth for me one who is to rule in Israel, whose origin is from of old, from ancient days. Therefore he shall give them up until the time when she who is in labor has brought forth; then the rest of his kindred shall return to the people of Israel. And he shall stand and feed his flock in the strength of the Lord, in the majesty of the name of the Lord his God. And they shall live secure, for now he shall be great to the ends of the earth; and he shall be the one of peace. If the Assyrians come into our land and tread upon our soil, we will raise against the seven shepherds and eight installed as rulers.

Leader: This candle we light today helps us to remember that Jesus Christ is the light of the world, and in him we find salvation.

People: **Let this light of salvation shine on us. Thanks be to God.**

Prayer

Our Father and our God, the author of everlasting life, the creator of all who are and everything that is, the giver of salvation, and the Father of our Lord and Savior, Jesus Christ, we gather to worship thee and to sing praises to thy name. In this Advent season prepare our hearts to receive the Savior. May he be born anew in each of us, and may he find a place to live in our lives, so that our faith becomes incarnational, a reality and not a theory, something that is seen in the world and not just read about in books.

So, we thank thee, gracious God, for this gift of the Savior. We are thankful for his wonderful birth, his winsome life, his marvelous teaching, his sacrificial death, and his glorious resurrection. We thank thee for all other wonderful gifts we receive from thee; family and friends, work and play, church and community, places of service and witness. Accept our thanksgiving for all thy gifts.

Continue to be at work in our lives. Mold us after the likeness of thy Son. Make us into his image. Enable us to reflect in our lives his love, mercy, grace, and forgiveness. Help us to be healers, helpers, lifters, and encouragers.

Guide us as a church, and bless the work we do here for thy kingdom, that we may be a blessing to others so that the lives of people the world over and the lives of those across the street may be blessed by thee.

Increase our faith, confirm our hope, and make us more loving and understanding.

Be with those of our church and community who have problems too great for them to solve and burdens too great for them to bear. Enable us to help them, and may they find their rest in thee. Be especially with the sick and those who mourn.

Bring peace, good will and understanding, sanity and hope to thy world, and we ask all of this in the name of thy well beloved Son and our Savior, Jesus Christ. Amen.

The People Of The Light, #3

Object: a manger Chrismon for the Chrismon tree

Okay, boys and girls, here we are now on the third Sunday in Advent. We are getting closer and closer to Christmas, and I want us to continue to think about the people of the light.

Today, I want you to look at this Chrismon from our tree. Who knows what this is? *(let them answer)* Yes, and this manger reminds us of what? *(let them answer)* It helps us think about Jesus being born in a manger.

The person we think about today is Mary, the mother of Jesus. When she was a very young woman she was told by an angel that she was going to have a baby, and this baby would be the Son of God.

Not only this, but because he would be God's Son, he would have very special work to do for God and God's people. Mary was told she should name her baby Jesus for he would save his people from their sins. He was born to be the Savior of the world.

This has many meanings. He saves us from the things we do which come between us and God and other people. Sometimes there are things we do which hurt another person, or which may hurt God, because he wants us to do better. Jesus helps us do better. He helps us love God and love other people, and not do things that would hurt them.

Then, he helps us be the best persons we can be. He helps us do good things and helpful things for God and for other people.

He makes our lives become the best lives they can possibly be, so that we can do all the things God wants us to do, and has made us able to do.

He gives us something good to live for, and we call this God's kingdom. It is God's rule in our lives. God is our leader. God loves us, blesses our lives, and helps us to live the best lives we can live.

This makes the world better. It helps all God's children. God helps the world through us and what we do.

Some day when we die, we will go to live with God forever in heaven, where God will love us and take care of us. All of this happens because Jesus is the Savior. He gives us God's gift of salvation.

Let Jesus, the Savior, live with you and in you, and he will always take care of you.

In The Darkness Of Fear, There Is The Light Of Joy

One cold Sunday afternoon in December, the congregation of a little Baptist church went over to the nearby river where they did their baptizing. They had several persons who were to be baptized that afternoon. There was one man who had some reservations about all this, as he faced the icy-cold water. He was a new convert and all this was foreign to him. He was, therefore, last in line. He noticed that when the first person came up out of the water, she quoted a Bible verse: "Bless the Lord, O my soul." Then a man was baptized, and he said, "The Lord is my shepherd." Then another man said, "I can do all things through Christ." Suddenly, it was his turn. He went under the water and came back up gasping for air. He did not know any verse to quote, so he looked around and simply announced to the crowd joyfully, "Merry Christmas, everyone!"

Here we are on the Sunday before Christmas. We have come most all the way through Advent. On these Sundays, we have been thinking together about the theme: The light of Bethlehem still shines. Today, I want us to focus our attention on this: In the darkness of fear, there is the light of joy.

From the earliest time, human beings have known fear, have experienced fear, have had to overcome fear. Far from being negative, fear can be a positive force in our lives because it can cause us to prepare, to get ready, to be on guard. But fear can also overwhelm us. It can immobilize us and paralyze us.

We need something that will enable us to face our fears, for still in our world today, in spite of all the advances that have been made, we are a people who are afraid.

I want to remind you that the light of Bethlehem still shines on us. As that great hymn tells us, "The hopes and fears of all the years are met in thee tonight."[1]

This is why Christmas is always such good news for us. It has a great message for us, "Be not afraid; for behold, I bring you good news of a great joy which will come to all the people."

The words from the Gospel according to Saint Luke, chapter 2, are some of the most beautiful words ever written. This is a story of such simple beauty and joy. It is a great human story into which the divine boldly comes.

Alan Culpepper, in *The New Interpreter's Bible*, says that after a long first chapter of Luke, we have in chapter 2 the birth of Jesus being related in just two verses, with only five setting the stage. In chapter 1, there are eighty verses, and we have this long account of the annunciation of the births of Jesus and John, with 23 verses being devoted to John's birth and his future role as a prophet and forerunner of the Messiah.[2]

What Saint Luke has given us, is the brief, plain, striking story of a young couple going on a journey and having a child late in the night.

A decree went out from Caesar Augustus that all people should take part in the world's first census. The purpose for that was the first systematic taxation. Everyone went back to their own hometowns to be registered.

Joseph and Mary went from Nazareth down south to Bethlehem, just a few miles below Jerusalem. Joseph was from that town, the city of David, and he was a descendant of Israel's greatest king.

While they were there, right after they got there, Mary had her baby. It must have been a time of fear for them, and yet, it was a time of joy as well.

> *The darkest time of the year,*
> *The poorest place in town,*
> *Cold, and a taste of fear,*
> *Man and woman alone.*
> *What can we hope for here?*
> *More light than we can learn,*
> *More wealth than we can treasure*
> *More love than we can earn,*
> *More peace than we can measure,*
> *Because one child is born.*[3]

Because this one child was born, we can face all our fears. We all have fears, in one form or another, at one time or another, in one way or another.

Even in the darkness of fear, the light of joy still shines.

Would you be willing to face these fears this morning and in this joyous season of the year?

I

Let this light of joy shine on you and let it be a surprise.

You can do that.

Saint Luke tells us there were shepherds out in the fields, keeping watch over their flocks. There, they had the surprise of a lifetime. Saint Luke writes, "An angel of the Lord appeared to them, and the glory of the Lord shone around them, and they were filled with fear."

I have been to that place where the shepherds were. It is a vast pasture area still today, where the winter rains cause grass to grow. Shepherds still take their sheep there to feed. You can stand down there in those fields and see Bethlehem on a distant hill.

In that place, the shepherds were surprised as "the glory of the Lord shone around them."

Most all of us here today — I dare say all of us — need this light of joy to shine on us — and we need to be surprised by it.

When our children were small, they would have a long list of things they wanted for Christmas. Down at the bottom of the list, they would write, "Lots of surprises."

That needs to be at the top of the list for all of us. That is one of our problems. How can we plan to be surprised?

A preacher went to see one of the families in his church. He was met at the door by a six-year-old boy who said, "Preacher, am I glad to see you. I have some good news. Daddy and I are taking mama to the hospital to get a baby. But don't tell her about it. We want it to be a surprise."

It is difficult to plan a surprise for yourself.

It is the kind of thing about which Yogi Berra would probably say, "Most surprises are unexpected."

Sometimes, the things we plan with the greatest detail, however, turn out to be a surprise.

At a little church, the pastor helped plan the Christmas pageant. They had several good rehearsals, and he talked to the children about their costumes. On the night of the performance, he was greeting the children as they arrived. He checked out each of them. He was surprised by three brothers, who were playing the Wise Men. They arrived, wearing raincoats, helmets, and pulling a water hose. The pastor said, "Hey, you are supposed to be wise men, not firemen." The brothers said, "We are wise men. Our dad told us the Wise Men came from afar."

I suppose our problem is we think we have to plan it all; even life's surprises. Maybe what we must do is stand back, catch our breath for a moment and let the glory of the Lord shine on us. Maybe we could dare to do that — open our lives up to some surprise by God and let God shine his light of joy on us, especially in those times when, like the shepherds, we are terrified.

That is when we need to be surprised most of all. In the darkness of fear, let the light of joy shine on you.

C. S. Lewis wrote a book titled *Surprised By Joy*. What a gift!

II

Let this light of joy give you courage.

You can do that also, if you will. Let this light of joy give you courage.

This was the message of the angel for the shepherds, "Be not afraid; for behold, I bring you good news of great joy which will come to all the people."

Did you get that? Do not be afraid. Why? Because of this good news of great joy.

It does not read, "Be not afraid ... be courageous instead, be brave instead, be strong instead." None of these human qualities are the antidote of fear. The opposite of fear, the antidote of fear, the cure of fear, is joy. The joy of Christmas will keep you from being afraid.

Armed with the joy of Christmas, this light of joy shining around you, you can stand against anything and everything which would threaten you.

One of this century's greatest theologians was Paul Tillich. He wrote a book titled *The Courage To Be*. He said in that book, "The courage to be is the ethical act in which man affirms his own being in spite of those elements of his experience that conflict with his essential self-affirmation."[4]

Courage means we know who we are in spite of everything we face, and we can face even those things which threaten to destroy us.

In December 1944, during the Battle of the Bulge, the German army surrounded some Americans in the village of Bastonge. The German commander sent a message telling the Americans to surrender. The American commander sent back a one-word message, "Nuts!" It was one of the greatest responses of military history.

That is the message of Christmas for every Herod and every heartache and every hatred and every hardship and everything which would destroy you — Nuts! Or, as the angel put it, "Be not afraid; for behold, I bring you good news of great joy which will come to all people."

A long time ago, on a little farm on a cold, dark night, a man asked his son to go out to the well and get a bucket of water. The boy was afraid of the dark. The man said, "Here, son, you take this lamp with you. You won't see the well at first, but you will have enough light for each step you take, and you will make it there a step at a time."

Let the light of Christmas give you courage.

III

Let this light enable you to accept the gift.

And this last thing you can do as well.

The angel told the shepherds, "To you is born this day in the city of David, a Savior, who is Christ the Lord."

Here is the key: the Savior is for you. That is why this light of joy gives us courage. It is because the source of our joy is Jesus Christ *himself*. It is because of the one who is the light of joy.

One of the great hymns we sing is "Joy to the world, the Lord is come! Let earth receive her King."[5]

Harry Emerson Fosdick was one of the greatest preachers in American history. One Christmas, at his Riverside Church in New York, he preached a sermon titled, "Christ Himself Is Christianity."[6]

He is the light of the world, and he is the light of joy.

This is your best gift at Christmas. He has come to save the world and he has come to save you.

This is why in the darkness of fear, the light of joy still smiles on us. It is a joy which casts out all fear.

Would you accept this gift this Christmas?

Sometimes, we do not know how to accept a gift.

A little boy was offered a gift of money from his uncle, who placed before the boy a penny, a nickel, a dime, a quarter, and a $1 bill. It was a difficult choice. The boy looked at that shiny penny and said, "I'll take that one and wrap it up in that one." He knew how to accept a gift.

Sometimes, it is easy for us to give, but not as easy to accept, a gift from someone else. We are gracious givers, but sometimes we are not gracious receivers.

Is it because we know we do not deserve what anyone else would do for us? Of course not. And that is just the point. A gift comes to us out of the love of the other person, and not because we deserve it or earn it. That is why it is a gift.

Christmas is a gift. The light of joy is a gift. Our Savior, Christ the Lord, is a gift.

Because of this gift, we can stand against, above, and even in the midst of, the darkness of fear.

Alex, The Life Of A Child, written by Frank Deford, tells the story of his daughter and her fight with cystic fibrosis. She died at the age of eight. During their last Christmas together, they go to church. The minister invites the children to come forward and place the figures in the manger scene. Alex felt she had missed Sunday school too much and did not want to go up, but she was called up to put the angel in place. In telling of this event, in that service, Frank Deford writes, "She beamed, popped right up, marched smartly to the crèche, took the angel, and tenderly placed it so it could look down protectively over the whole scene." Then she came back and they knew it was her last Christmas, but they talked later of her being their angel.[7] May we all have such faith.

Would you accept the gift of Christmas joy, the gift of Christ the Lord, the gift of a Savior? If you would, you would then be able to face all that life brings your way.

In the darkness of fear, the light of joy still shines.

---

1. Phillips Brooks, "O Little Town Of Bethlehem," *The United Methodist Hymnal* (Nashville: The United Methodist Publishing House, 1989), p. 230.

2. R. Alan Culpepper, "The Gospel Of Luke," *The New Interpreter's Bible*, Vol. IX (Nashville: Abingdon Press, 1995), p. 62.

3. Christopher Fry, *McCall's* magazine, December 1968, quoted by David A. MacLennan, *Sermons Of Faith And Hope* (Valley Forge, Pennsylvania: Judson Press, 1971), p. 10.

4. Paul Tillich, *The Courage To Be* (New Haven and London: Yale University Press, 1952), p. 3.

5. Isaac Watts, "Joy To The World," *The United Methodist Hymnal* (Nashville: The United Methodist Publishing House, 1989), p. 246.

6. Harry Emerson Fosdick, *On Being Fit To Live With* (New York and London: Harper And Brothers, 1946), p. 185.

7. Frank Deford, *Alex, The Life Of A Child*, for The Cystic Fibrosis Foundation (Washington, D.C.: Viking Press, 1983), p. 120.

Advent 4
Candlelighting and Prayer

Lighting Of The Fourth Advent Candle

Scripture Reading — Isaiah 55:6-9, 12-13

Seek the Lord while he may be found, call upon him while he is near; let the wicked forsake their way, and the unrighteous their thoughts; let them return to the Lord, that he may have mercy on them, and to our God, for he will abundantly pardon. For my thoughts are not your thoughts, nor are your ways my ways, says the Lord. For as the heavens are higher than the earth, so are my ways higher than your ways and my thoughts than your thoughts.... For you shall go out in joy, and be led back in peace; the mountains and the hills before you shall burst into song, and all the trees of the field shall clap their hands. Instead of the thorn shall come up the cypress; instead of the brier shall come up the myrtle; and it shall be to the Lord for a memorial, for an everlasting sign that shall not be cut off.

Leader: This candle we light today helps us to remember that Jesus Christ is the light of the world, and in him we find joy.

People: **Let this light of joy shine on us. Thanks be to God.**

Prayer

Almighty God, our Heavenly Father, whom we have come to know in thy Son, Jesus Christ, who is the way, the truth, and the life, continue to lead us in this Advent season that we will know the joy of our Lord. May we walk in his ways.

50

Continue to lead us along the way to Bethlehem, that we would all be able to find that place, and have the light of Bethlehem shine on each of us. In this way, O God, we know we will find life, and find it abundantly.

Receive our hymns of praise today, O God, and our prayers of thanksgiving for all thou hast done for us. We thank thee for all good gifts, and that we are thy children, the subjects of thy love and care. Most of all we thank thee for the gift of thy Son and our Savior, who was born into this world that we might know the true meaning of hope, life, salvation, and joy.

We are thankful for this thy church, for its mission and ministry, and for the vital part played in it by every member of this church. Continue to call forth from us our self-giving devotion, that we would give the best we have to the highest we know.

Forgive our sins and by thy grace cause us to rise above all that would hold us down. Give us courage, strength, and endurance.

Lead us in the ways of peace. Guide the leaders of the world. Protect us in times of war, and protect all the great people of the world, and we will give thee all honor, praise, and glory, for we pray in the name of thy Son, Jesus Christ. Amen.

Advent 4
Children's Message

The People Of The Light, #4

Object: a hammer Chrismon to put on the Chrismon tree

Boys and girls, I am so glad all of you have come to church today. This is the fourth Sunday in Advent, and we are really close to Christmas now. It will be here in just a few days. We have been thinking together about the people of the light.

Someone tell us about this Chrismon. Yes, it is a hammer. This reminds us that the earthly father of Jesus was Joseph. He was a carpenter. He worked in the carpenter's shop in the town of Nazareth. The angel of the Lord told him to take Mary to be his wife, even though she was already going to have this baby, because the baby was going to be God's Son.

Joseph belonged to the same family as King David. He was a descendant of David. The Roman government decided that every person was to be enrolled in the first census in history. That meant each family had to return to the man's hometown to sign up in this census. Joseph took Mary with him for the long journey from Nazareth down to Bethlehem. Bethlehem was where David was from, and so it was also the home for Joseph's family. That is the place where Jesus was born.

Joseph was a person of the light because he helped Mary raise Jesus. He took care of him from the very beginning. He took Mary and the baby Jesus away to Egypt to protect him from the meanness of old King Herod. Then, he took them back home to Nazareth, there he raised Jesus in the carpenter's shop. Jesus grew up to be strong and brave because of Joseph.

Joseph shared with Mary the joy of having this baby born into their little family. Together they welcomed him, received him, nourished him, took care of him, raised him, taught him their scriptures, raised him in the synagogue in their town, and lived before him as an example of how a person loves and serves God.

When Jesus was twelve years old, they took him to the temple in Jerusalem for his bar-mitzvah. When they started home, they realized he was not with them. They went back and found him talking with the teachers. He said to them, "Didn't you know I must be about my Father's business?" meaning God's business, the work God wanted him to do. I believe one reason Jesus grew up thinking this way, and why he became the man he was, was because of the kind of good man Joseph was, and the example he set for young Jesus. Jesus grew up knowing the joy of serving God, his heavenly Father. He learned that from Joseph, his earthly father.

You can be a person of light, also, and you will discover the joy of serving God.

In The Darkness Of Anxiety, There Is The Light Of Peace

On a recent Sunday night, my wife and I went to a nearby church for their "Bethlehem Walk." Each year, they re-create the town of Bethlehem with shops, sheep, Roman soldiers, a prophet crying out in the street who looked, strangely enough, like the pastor of the church, and a young couple with a new baby out in an animal shed.

We arrived early so we would not have to wait in line long. That probably does not make sense, since we were in line long, but not a long line being at the front of it. As we stood there waiting, after having hurried, we suddenly saw a bright shooting star streaking across the sky. It was a striking reminder of another Bethlehem and another star and other people who hurried about on a night, long ago.

When we left, that line was unbelievably long, with people rushing to get in.

Thinking about this later, I wondered how different that Bethlehem was from one so long ago. I thought about people anxiously lining up to get into Bethlehem, hoping to find some sense of peace.

That we live in a time of great anxiety is not even debatable. It is ironic that all the things we have done, invented, and produced, have not reduced anxiety at all. In fact, there is every reason to believe that our great technological advances have increased anxiety, rather than reducing it.

There was a report in the news about a bank that had some uncertainty about their computer system as the year 2000 approached. They decided to test it, and prepared overdraft statements with dates on them well beyond the year 2000. They were relieved to find their systems worked perfectly. There was no problem. Well, there was one problem. Some person in the bank mailed them out to its customers.

There was another report in the news that a recent study indicated that people who spend a lot of time chatting on the internet are experiencing increased stress and anxiety because of decreased human contact.

Here we are on Christmas Eve. We come here looking for something that belongs to a simpler time, something less complicated, something that is real and true and good. We want to recapture something we are sometimes afraid we have lost.

We come seeking faith and goodness and God. We turn back to a manger, a baby, and good news of great joy, and peace on earth and in our lives.

Throughout this Advent season, we have been thinking together about this theme: The light of Bethlehem still shines on. Tonight, we turn to this: In the darkness of anxiety, there is the light of peace.

This is the night. "The hopes and fears of all the years, are met in thee tonight."[1]

This is Bethlehem for us. We are here tonight in Bethlehem, and there is a light that shines in this darkness that surrounds us. It is the light of Christ, the light of peace. In the darkness of anxiety, the light of peace still shines on us.

Saint Luke tells us there were shepherds out in the fields, keeping watch over their flocks.

When the angel of the Lord appeared to them, they were told a Savior had been born in Bethlehem. The angel said to the shepherds, "This will be a sign for you: you will find a babe wrapped in swaddling cloths and lying in a manger." And then they heard a group of angels singing, "Glory to God in the highest, and on earth peace among men with whom he is pleased." When the angels went away, the shepherds said, "Let us go over to Bethlehem and see this thing that has happened, which the Lord has made known to us." Then the shepherds went to Bethlehem with haste.

We come to Christmas with a good deal of haste. We hurry along toward it. Before we know it, it has come and gone and we have missed it.

There is always the danger that in all this we miss the thing we are searching for most, the peace of God which comes to us only from the Prince of Peace.

From this wonderful Christmas story, we have heard tonight, let me make some suggestions for all of us who need to find the light of peace in the darkness of anxiety.

First, think about this:

I

Look for signs of God's peace.

In a world like ours, you have to look.

The angel of the Lord said to the shepherds, "Be not afraid; for behold, I bring you good news of great joy which will come to all the people; for to you is born this day in the city of David a Savior, who is Christ the Lord. And this will be a sign for you: you will find a babe wrapped in swaddling cloths and lying in a manger."

The birth of that child was a sign of God's love, mercy, and grace; a sign of God's peace.

In today's world, we do not always look at the birth of a child in this way, for much of our world is cold and uncaring.

In a college sociology class, the professor said, "Somewhere in this world, there is a woman having a baby every three seconds. What can we do about it?" One student spoke up and said, "We've got to find that woman and stop her!"

What we must do is find that baby boy born in a manger and wrapped in bands of cloth.

In a world like ours, you have to look for signs of God's peace, but you do not have to look far. Signs of God's peace are all around.

God's graceful Son was born in Bethlehem, and when he entered the world, he brought God's grace with him. He was the embodiment of God's peace. They called him, "The Prince of Peace."

If we look, we will find him.

The angel of the Lord said, "You will find a babe."

Take that as a personal statement to you. You will find him.

Where will we find him? We will find him in the common, everyday things of life.

A family waited anxiously in the hospital while a loved one hovered between life and death. The family's pastor was there with them. One man in that family, who was always suspicious of religion, said to him, "Okay, preacher, tell me now. Where is your God at a time like this?" A nurse, who had been helping their family member, walked by. The pastor pointed to her and said, "There goes God. God is here in the touch of that nurse."

You need to look for signs of God's peace in the kindness of others, in the generosity of friends, in the lives of fellow Christians, and in the mission of the church.

Then, second, move on to this:

II

Accept the promise of God's peace.

In a world like ours, we need to accept it.

The shepherds heard this wonderful anthem sung by a multitude of heavenly host, "Glory to God in the highest, and on earth, peace among men with whom he is pleased."

The anthem they sang was a promise from God, a promise of peace. Glory to God, because he is sending his Son to bring peace, to embody peace, to proclaim peace, and to offer peace.

In this Christmas season, would you accept the promise of peace for yourself?

Our entire world needs it greatly. The world cries out for peace and justice. Suffering people all over the world need and deserve peace.

All of us who gather here tonight need peace.

God has pronounced to us in the coming of his Son his peace, and God gives it to us through Jesus.

Sometimes we can miss it during Christmas.

One Christmas, our church choir went caroling. After going to several homes, they came by to see us. We stood in the doorway as they sang. Then, a lady in the choir led us all in prayer. Right in the middle of her prayer, I heard our cat come running through the house. It was a bitter, cold night, and we had decided to keep him inside, but here he came, headed for the open front door. I yelled out in the middle of her prayer, "Grab the cat, quick!" That lady never did forgive me for that.

We get all caught up in Christmas, and if we are not careful, we miss the point of it. You can decide for yourself tonight that you will accept the promise of God's peace.

A young lady was on her way to China where she would serve as a missionary, teaching in a Christian school. She had to travel by boat, and she found the voyage to be long and difficult. She had many concerns about this and wondered how she would be able to survive there. One night, she had a dream in which she was standing on a plank out in the ocean. In her dream, God told her to start walking toward China. She said she could not do it. She could not walk on water. But the voice insisted, so she stepped out to the end of the plank and another plank appeared. Each time she reached the end of one plank, another was there. When she woke up, she accepted this dream as a promise from God. She was able to carry on because of that promise.[2]

That promise has been made to you. Accept the promise of God's peace.

Then, third, finally turn to this:

III

Put yourself in the place of God's peace.

In a world like ours, we have no other choice.

When the angels went away, the shepherds said to each other, "Let us go over to Bethlehem and see this thing that has happened, which the Lord has made known to us."

The shepherds knew they had to do something. This babe had come to them, but they had to go right then to the place where he was.

It comes down to this: Are you willing to go to the place where this child is, the place where you find God's peace?

We have put ourselves in all kinds of other places, sometimes at great expense, and we did not find it there. Having tried everything else in an attempt to alleviate our anxiety, I wonder now, would we try God?

Some do this in a glib sort of way. They have been into tennis, and into jogging, and into therapy, and into various forms of drugs. They think, "I'll try God now," in the way they might try on a pair of shoes. That is not what I mean.

I mean, would you put yourself in the place of God's peace, by putting your life in God's hands?

We had a replica town of Bethlehem at a church I once served. One Christmas Eve, we were going to leave our service in the sanctuary and go out to the manger where the holy family and some unholy looking shepherds waited on us. The notice in our bulletin was supposed to say, "Recessional To The Manger." What it actually said was, "Recessional To The Manager." I thought that was a wonderful mistake, and one that told the way it should be.

You need to let God be the one who manages your life. That is the only way any of us will find any peace at all.

You can put yourself in God's hands by taking this newborn babe in your hands.

Our son and his wife have two children. When their son was two, their nephew came over to watch the children, so the parents could go out. The nephew had the phone number of his grandmother so he could call her if he needed to do so. Things went fine, but after a while he called his grandma and said, "I have done everything on the list, everything I am supposed to do. I changed him, put pajamas on him, gave him his milk, and he's just standing in the middle of the floor, looking up at me." His grandmother said, "Tad, pick him up."

Do not just look at baby Jesus in the manger and think how nice it all is. Pick him up. Embrace him. Make him your own.

Can you imagine those shepherds gathering around the holy family, some kneeling, some peeping over at that little boy? Can you imagine Mary saying to them, "Go ahead. Pick him up. Embrace him!"

You do that and the light of peace will shine on you, and you will have the peace of God which passes all understanding.

---

1. Phillips Brooks, "O Little Town Of Bethlehem," *The United Methodist Hymnal* (Nashville: The United Methodist Publishing House, 1989), p. 230.

2. Robert C. Morgan, *Lift High The Cross* (Nashville: Abingdon Press, 1995), p. 5.

Lighting Of The Christ Candle

Scripture Reading — Isaiah 65:17-25

For I am about to create new heavens and a new earth; the former things shall not be remembered or come to mind. But be glad and rejoice forever in what I am creating; for I am about to create Jerusalem as a joy, and its people as a delight. I will rejoice in Jerusalem, and delight in my people; no more shall the sound of weeping be heard in it, or the cry of distress. No more shall there be in it an infant that lives but a few days, or an old person who does not live out a lifetime; for one who dies at a hundred years will be considered a youth, and one who falls short of a hundred will be considered accursed. They shall build houses and inhabit them; they shall plant vineyards and eat their fruit. They shall not build and another inhabit; they shall not plant and another eat; for like the days of a tree shall the days of my people be, and my chosen shall long enjoy the work of their hands. They shall not labor in vain, or bear children for calamity; for they shall be offspring blessed by the Lord — and their descendants as well. Before they call I will answer, while they are yet speaking I will hear. The wolf and the lamb shall feed together, the lion shall eat straw like the ox; but the serpent — its food shall be dust! They shall not hurt or destroy on all my holy mountain, says the Lord.

Leader: This candle we light tonight helps us remember that Jesus Christ is the light of the world, and in him we find peace.

People: **Let this light of peace shine within us. Thanks be to God.**

Prayer

O God our Father, who has sent thy Son to be the Savior of the world, we pray that on this night our hearts and lives will be open to receiving him anew. May he be born in us again, and may we be protected from being too proud to kneel down to this Child and submit our lives to him and his rule in us.

We know, Father, that he is the hope of the world, and that the only real peace for anyone, anywhere is found in him. We pray for thy blessings upon the world this night, that all the world may know of thy transforming grace and thy love expressed in the life of this, thy Son.

Bless people everywhere tonight, in big cities and in small towns and villages. Bless rich people and poor people, and all us people in between. Bless educated people and simple people. Bless people who work in office buildings and factories, mills, stores, and shepherds' fields and people who do not work at all. Bless people who live in fine homes, cabins, apartments, and mansions and people who live out on the streets.

Into the lives of all these people, and into our lives, may the newborn king come marching. May this child grow up in us to become our master. While we marvel at his birth may we hurry to see that the real mystery is how he leads and rules, delivers and helps, heals and forgives, and loves and challenges us today. Then may we give ourselves to him anew as a part of our Christmas. May our response to this best gift be the giving of our hearts to him.

Merciful God, forgive us, because that is why he came, and give us faith, hope, peace, joy, a purpose for living, salvation. Call from us our finest service for thy kingdom, because that is why he came.

We make this our prayer this holy night in his holy name. Amen.

Christmas Eve
Children's Message

The People Of The Light, #5

Object: a gold key Chrismon to put on the Chrismon tree

This is the night, boys and girls. This is what we have been waiting for. I am so glad you have come to church tonight, because this is the most important night. It is the night of the Savior's birth.

I want us to think about the innkeeper. We know that when Joseph and Mary came into Bethlehem, they went to the inn, a hotel. But, when they knocked on the door, the innkeeper, the man who owned the hotel, told them he had no room, no place for them to stay. It was not his fault, and he was not being mean. It was just that all the rooms were filled with other people. But, he had a good idea. He told them they could stay in the stable. So he took them downstairs to the basement where a place for the animals had been dug out of the ground. It was probably even warmer than the hotel, and he let them spend the night there. That is where Jesus was born.

Look over on our Chrismon tree. Do you see a gold key? That key reminds us of the door to the stable which was opened up for Jesus and his family.

The innkeeper was one of the people of the light, because he opened up a place where Jesus could be born.

You can be a person of light if you will open up a place where Jesus can live. You can turn the key to your heart and open up the door to your heart and your life and let Jesus live in you.

Tonight, on this Christmas Eve, the best gift we receive is the gift of Jesus Christ. He is why we are here. You know that he is the key to everything for us. When we turn the key and open our lives to him, then he turns the key and opens up for us the very best life we can possibly live.

In The Darkness Of Uncertainty, There Is The Light Of Wonder

William Sloane Coffin, Jr., was, for several years, the pastor at Riverside Church in New York City. In his autobiography, he told of going back to France and visiting some of the places where he had been in World War II. One of those places was the town of Sainte-Mère-Eglise. The 82nd Airborn Division had dropped into that town.

While there for his visit, the mayor showed William around. They went inside the village church. The mayor pointed to a beautiful stained-glass window that depicted the 82nd Division parachuting into the town. On the window above the paratroopers, was the Virgin Mary with the Christ Child. The mayor said, "We designed the window like this so we might never forget that night."[1]

When I read that, I remembered seeing that scene in the movie, *The Longest Day.* I remember how one parachute caught on the steeple of the church and one soldier was hanging there. It was an unforgettable scene.

I also remembered talking with a member of the church I served who was in that parachute jump. He had seen the movie, also. But, he did not need to see it to remember what happened that day, for he had experienced it. He had been there that day and that experience had been burned into his soul.

Here we are now on the other side of Christmas, with the feeling that it has come and gone. It is something we have done, and unfortunately for many of us, there is a sense of relief that it is over and also a bit of a let-down that nothing more has come about in our lives because of it.

On this side of Christmas we can hold onto the wonder of it all. Let the truth of what has happened in the great Christ event be for you an experience that has been burned into your soul.

I would like for us to think together about this: In the darkness of uncertainty, there is the light of wonder.

On this side of Christmas, the light of Bethlehem still shines on. Even though the times in which we live are uncertain, as all times are, and even though our own personal lives have times of uncertainty, the light of Bethlehem still shines. Let the light of wonder still shine upon you.

For those people who gathered there in Bethlehem on that night so long ago, there was a sense of wonder at the things they had heard, seen, and experienced. It was a night like no other, one they would never forget. We have not forgotten it, either.

Saint Luke tells us that when the shepherds came into town and found the child they "made known the saying which had been told them." They shared what they had heard from the angels, ... and all who heard it wondered at what the shepherds told them.

I have no way of knowing what happened to those shepherds after that night. It is difficult for me to imagine them ever getting over it. I cannot help but believe that they always remembered it, held onto it, and kept alive in their hearts the wonder of it. Perhaps, some of them were still around when Jesus came to Jerusalem, many years later. I can almost see them saying to each other, "Remember that night long ago. We knew then there was something special about him, and now here he is."

I know Mary and Joseph held onto the wonder of that night. Parents always hold on to the wonder of birth, and this birth was a special birth. Saint Luke said Mary "... kept all these things, pondering them in her heart."

Saint Luke wrote that "... the shepherds returned, glorifying and praising God for all they had heard and seen, as it had been told them." This experience turned them toward God. They worshiped God because of what had taken place.

In the experience of these people, caught up in the first Christmas, we see some hints for ourselves.

They lived in times more uncertain than our own. Those were dangerous times. They had none of the advantages and safeguards we have today. Human life was not worth much. The domination of Rome made life uncertain at best.

Yet, in spite of this, their lives were filled with wonder.

Do you feel like you are up against a wall? Do you think your life is filled with uncertainty and the darkness of it has fallen upon you? Let the light of wonder shine upon you and in you. Remember the things we see in this story:

I

Let the song of the angels continue to fill your heart.

When the shepherds came to Bethlehem, their hearts were full of what they had heard from the angels. It was because of that announcement that they said to each other, "Let us go over to Bethlehem and see this thing that has happened." When they got there, they shared what they had been told. From then on, the rest of their lives there must have been a song in their hearts.

Some of us need to catch that now. All of us need this song in our hearts, the song of the angels, the great anthem of Christmas.

What if we could take Christmas to heart? What if we could make it a part of us and internalize all of this?

Maybe that would keep us from making Christmas something we can merely find our way through and then pack up in a box and put away until next year.

When we do that, Christmas is something we get over quickly.

A preacher went to see an older lady in his church. She had not been well, so he wanted to check on her. As they talked, he noticed a bowl of peanuts on a table by the chair where he sat. He ate one and then another. Soon, they were all gone. He said to her, "Oh, I'm sorry. I've eaten all your peanuts." She replied, "That's okay. I've already eaten the chocolate off them. That's the only part of them I could have."

Some of us live like someone has eaten the chocolate off our peanuts, licked the stripe off our candy cane, or popped our little bubble. Instead of being on top of the world, we live down in the dumps.

We let the uncertainty of life overwhelm us, but it does not have to be that way. Let the song of the angels continue to fill your heart.

Remember that Jesus was born into a world that was down in the dumps, filled with fear, frustration, suffering, and uncertainty. He was born to be the light of the world, in a very dark time.

Several years ago, on Christmas Eve, I drove through the streets of our town and watched the falling snow. I looked at every house and saw trees lit up, candles in the windows, and I listened to Christmas music on the radio. I became caught up in the wonder of Christmas. Yet, I went by homes where I knew there had been pain, sorrow, and suffering. I found myself saying, "God, bless the people in that house." Then, I would come to another home up the street and I would say, "God, bless the people in that house." The beauty, serenity, and the appealing thoughts of Christmas, with thoughts of quiet streets in Bethlehem, do not get our minds off the way life is. They remind us of life and the great needs all of us have, the great problems all of us face.

That is what this little boy Jesus is all about. Let the song of the angels continue to fill your heart — "Glory to God in the highest, peace on earth, good will among men."

Remember this as well:

II

Let the light of the star continue to shine in you.

The light of the star pointed to where Jesus was to be found. Like the Wise Men from the east, the shepherds must have followed the light of the star to where he was.

Saint John began his Gospel by writing, "In him was life, and the life was the light of men. The light shines in the darkness, and the darkness has not overcome it."

The light of the star still points to where he is to be found, and it is a reminder of him who is the light of the world.

He is the light which shines upon us and warms us with the warmth of God's love.

He is the light which shines around us to light up the road we travel, to help us find our way.

He is the light which shines through us, and calls us to be light and live light and share light, even when there is darkness all around.

There is still a great deal of darkness in this world. God calls us to be people of the light.

During the fourteenth century, the Black Death swept across Europe, taking the lives of thousands of people. In some towns, every person died. Many people locked themselves up in their homes, hoping to avoid the illness. On Christmas Eve, in the year 1353, in the town of Goldberg, Germany, there was a man who thought he must be the last person alive. He remembered the joy of other Christmas seasons. He decided that with his family and friends gone, he did not want to live any longer. He walked out into the street to face death. As he walked along, he sang a Christmas song, and was surprised that soon another voice joined his own. Several people came out and joined him, and when they reached the end of the street, they found they had a group of 25 men, women, and children. They all sang together. Then, they returned to their homes and began to put their lives back together again. The worst had passed. A tradition was begun there that lasted for centuries. Each Christmas Eve, the people march through the streets and sing these words:

> *To us this day is born a child.*
> *God with us.*
> *His mother is a virgin mild.*
> *God with us. God with us.*
> *Against us who dare be?*[2]

In spite of the darkness that is in the world, this light can shine in us. It must shine in us and we must let it shine. We must let it shine because there is still much darkness that would attempt to stand against God.

The light of Christ shines in the midst of darkness, a darkness which cannot overcome the light.

Let the light of the star, the light of wonder, shine in you.

Then, finally, this:

III

Let the wonder of his birth continue to transform you. This is also something about Christmas we need to take with us.

69

The shepherds made known all they had heard. Saint Luke tells us "all who heard it wondered at what the shepherds told them." Then, the shepherds went away praising God for all they had heard and seen.

We can let the good news of Christmas, and the joy of Christmas fill our lives with a sense of wonder which we can take away with us.

This sense of wonder can transform our lives and our living and give us a new purpose, a new direction, a new destiny.

This will lift our lives and our living above the ordinary and the mundane.

A farm couple was sitting in front of the fire one night. The wife said, "Jed, I think it's raining. Why don't you go see?" Without looking up, Jed replied, "Ah, just leave me alone. Why don't you just call in the dog and see if he's wet?"

Wouldn't you hate to live with that kind of attitude? We do not have to live that way. We can let the wonder of the birth of Christ transform us and our living.

Some of you will remember the first of the great disaster movies, *The Poseidon Adventure*. It is still shown on television. It was the story of a ship that was turned upside down by a storm at sea. The movie centered around the surviving passengers searching for a way out of the ship. One of the central characters, the Reverend Scott, found a way to search for an escape from the rising waters within the ship. He climbed up a Christmas tree and tried to get others to follow him up to the next level of the ship. He kept calling them, "Come on up. It's this way." Only a few would go with him. The others were afraid and one shouted back at him, "Why don't you mind your own business?" He was. He was trying to save them.

When I saw that, I could not help but think of how Jesus, the one born to be a king, dared to climb the tree in order to save us, and how he calls back to us, "It's this way."

In all the uncertainties of your own life, take this away from Christmas with you. In the darkness of uncertainty, let the light of wonder shine on you. It will fill your life with joy and wonder.

1. William Sloane Coffin, Jr., *Once To Every Man* (New York: Atheneum, 1978), p. 85.

2. Donald J. Shelby, "King Of The Nations, Their Desire And Cornerstone," *Santa Monica Sermons*, December 4 (Santa Monica, California: First United Methodist Church, 1983), p. 7.

Christmas 1
Candlelighting and Prayer

Lighting Of The Christ Candle

Scripture Reading — Isaiah 9:2-7

The people who walked in darkness have seen a great light; those who lived in a land of deep darkness — on them light has shined. You have multiplied the nation, you have increased its joy; then rejoice before you as with joy at the harvest, as people exult when dividing plunder. For the yoke of their burden, and the bar across their shoulders, the rod of their oppressor, you have broken as on the day of Midian. For all the boots of the tramping warriors and all the garments rolled in blood shall be burned as fuel for the fire. For a child has been born for us, a son given to us; authority rests upon his shoulders; and he is named Wonderful Counselor, Mighty God, Everlasting Father, Prince of Peace. His authority shall grow continually, and there shall be endless peace for the throne of David and his kingdom. He will establish and uphold it with justice and with righteousness from this time onward and forevermore. The zeal of the Lord of hosts will do this.

Leader: This candle we light today helps us remember that Jesus Christ is the light of the world, and in him we experience wonder.

People: **Let this light of wonder shine within us. Thanks be to God.**

Prayer

O Father, we gather on this glad day to sing praises to thy name for the miracle of Christmas and the Savior's birth. We rejoice that once again we have been able to celebrate his coming to us, and that we have experienced him anew. So receive our worship today and may all we do bring glory to thee.

Help us, O God, to be people who have our lives changed because of Christmas. Keep us from ever again being the way we used to be and traveling the roads we used to travel. Instead, may we return to our lives rejoicing and filled with wonder over this great thing we have seen take place.

We thank thee for all that this Christmas has meant to us, and for the knowledge most of all that the Savior has come. We also thank thee for the little human kindnesses done for us, the gifts we have received, the joys shared, the private and public celebrations, and even more for gifts we have given and the joys we have been able to bring into the lives of others. We are thankful for all these things because they remind us of thy love for us, and the great divine generosity we have experienced because Jesus has been born into this world and into our lives.

Help us, then, to be people who share this good news with the rest of the world, the people across the street and the people across the earth. Give us a new sense of mission and ministry. Bless the work and the witness of our church. Help us to seek and find new opportunities for service and to build thy kingdom in the lives of people.

Forgive us when we fall short, and when we fail, either by our willful disobedience or in times when we simply miss the mark. Put a new and right spirit within us. Give us faith, and fill us with the confident assurance of the people of God.

Bless all who suffer the world over and those we know and love who are sick, alone, afraid. Comfort them and enable us to comfort them. For we make our prayer in Jesus' name. Amen.

Christmas 1
Children's Message

The People Of The Light, #6

Object: a shepherd's staff Chrismon to put on the Chrismon tree

Well, boys and girls, I hope all of you had a wonderful Christmas. But it is not over yet. It is still going on. Today we are going to continue looking at the people of the light, those people who were a part of the first Christmas.

I want us to look at the shepherds. There were a number of people who came to see Jesus. Some of those were the shepherds. They raised sheep, and they lived in and around Bethlehem. There's a very large pasture area there near town. I have been there and have seen it. That is probably where the shepherds were that night Jesus was born. That place is called shepherds' fields.

It was to these shepherds that the good news of Jesus' birth came on that night. When they heard it, they were at first afraid. When the angels sang out, the shepherds were filled with fear. But later they believed, and they went into Bethlehem to see this wonderful thing that had taken place, the birth of the Savior.

Not only did they believe, they were also happy about it, and they told everyone what they had been told. They shared what the angels sang out to them.

Then, they rejoiced and praised God when they left the manger. They celebrated.

That is what we are supposed to do. Today, we are the people of the light, and because of Christmas we are to believe, tell the good news, rejoice, and worship God.

We have a Chrismon to remind us of this. Who can see it? That's right, the shepherd's staff. It also looks like a candy cane, which is why we have them at Christmas. Turn it upside down and you have the letter "J" for Jesus.

I want you to be a person who is like the shepherds. I want you to help spread the news.

In The Darkness Of Suspicion, There Is The Light Of Devotion

It was a few days after Christmas. A mother was busy cleaning up the den, putting everything away, taking the Christmas tree down. Her son came in and saw her and said, "Mama, what are you doing?" She said, "I'm putting all our Christmas stuff away." He asked in reply, "Why are you doing that?" She answered, "So everything will be back to normal again." His response to that was, "Mama, I don't want things to get back to normal again."

On this second Sunday after Christmas, we have the thought in our minds that Christmas is over. There is often the urge, the desire, to pack everything up and get it out of the way. But, sometimes, I think we rush away from it too quickly, do too good a job at cleaning up after it, and in that we run the risk of removing it from our lives.

What if after Christmas we could keep life from getting back to normal again? What if we could really hang onto it and take it with us into these good days ahead of us in the new year?

I want to suggest to us today that we can do just that. By that, I do not mean that everything is going to be perfect, or always go our way. Nor do I mean we will be able to escape the same routine, the same schedule, the same duties, we have had to struggle with before. But, I would suggest that there ought to be something different about us because we have been able to see again a star of wonder, to hear again the angels sing, to hear again the cry of a babe, and have our hearts strangely warmed because God has bent low to the earth, again.

Today, I remind us of the story of the visit of the Magi, three Wise Men from the east, to the holy family in Bethlehem.

We have been thinking during these weeks about the theme: The light of Bethlehem still shines on. Today, we come finally to this: In the darkness of suspicion, there is the light of devotion.

Traditionally, the Christian church has remembered the visit of the Magi twelve days after Christmas, on the day of Epiphany.

This is a great story we heave heard today. These three men came into Jerusalem looking for a king. They met another king who immediately felt threatened when he found out what they were doing there. He became suspicious of them and this new king. He began to plot the death of any and all who would claim any kind of royalty. In that darkness of suspicion, the light of devotion was shining. The Wise Men were very wise. They came to give their devotion to the new king and would not be turned aside.

In our world today, there is still a good bit of suspicion. It can poison relationships, goals, noble-endeavors, groups, and ideals. In the darkness of suspicion, let the light of devotion still shine on you.

Hang onto this as we move away from Christmas.

One year, as we were putting things away after Christmas, my wife said, "Well, Christmas is about over." Our daughter replied, "Yes, but we still have the memories."

Let the memory of that night and those days so long ago continue to live in your heart.

Remember these things about the visit of the Magi and their devotion:

I

Keep Christ as the object of your devotion.

We see in those three men who came from so far away that he was just that for them. He was the object of their devotion.

Matthew tells us that the Magi came from the east to Jerusalem. They had one question on their minds, "Where is he who has been born king of the Jews? For we have seen his star in the East, and have come to worship him." Some translations read, "we have come to pay him homage." The point is clear. They came all that way for one reason and one reason only, to worship him, to make him the object of their devotion.

This is one of those things we must see. If we do not see this, we do not see Christmas, we do not understand it, and it makes no sense at all. If we do not see this, we will soon forget it and what it does.

Two couples were walking through the mall. They were talking about their church. One of the men was going to say something about the lady who was to teach their class the next Sunday. He turned to his wife and said, "What's the name? I don't remember like I used to." Then, he said to the other man, "Give me some help. Her name is like a flower." His friend said, "Violet, Rose." The first man replied, "That's it. Now, Rose, what is the name of the lady who teaches our class?"

Don't forget, "There is a name that is above every name." We are told "Call his name Jesus, for he shall save his people from their sins."

Christmas is the celebration of the birth of the one born to be king of all creation and king of all the creatures.

Take this with you into this new year. If you want your life to be better in the new year, keep Christ as the object of your devotion.

A pastor went to see a couple in his church. It was early March. As he sat in their den with them, he noticed a Christmas ornament hanging from a bookshelf. The lady saw him look at it and she said, "No, we did not forget. Every year when I put all the decorations away, I choose one to leave behind on purpose to remind me that Christmas is not just one day, or one season. For me, Christmas is a lifetime. That ornament is a reminder that Jesus walks with me every day."[1]

My wife and I have a collection of manger scenes. One of them we bought in Bethlehem. We never pack it away. It stays out all the year through. It is a reminder of the one born to be the object of our devotion.

Then, move on to something else:

II

Give to him the best that you have.

Keep Christ as the object of your devotion, and therefore give to him the best that you have.

77

Because the Magi, the three kings, paid homage to this new king, because they worshiped him, they presented to him their gifts of gold, frankincense, and myrrh. Gold was a gift fit for a king. It was costly, treasured, and sought after, and given to a baby king. Frankincense was an expensive fragrance, representing a personal treasure. It was a fine perfume. Myrrh was a precious ointment used in the preparation for death. It was tinged with sadness. All of these gifts were expensive treasures in that day and in that part of the world. Each of those men brought to the one they worshiped, the best they had to offer him. This was a sign of their dedication. Just as their kneeling was a sign of their homage, so were these gifts a sign of their dedication. It was also, I believe, a statement about their priorities.

Who and what do you really put in first place? I wonder, could any of us, or all of us, dare to do what these men did? Would you dare to give to Christ, the king, the best thing you have, the most expensive thing, the best part of you?

I wonder would you give the best you have, and if you did, what might that be? What might you be able to give to him in the year ahead?

Just before I was to speak at a lunch meeting, the person who was seated next to me shared a story that I then shared with the audience. It was about this group of ladies arriving in heaven. Saint Peter was questioning them and telling them they had to prove they were Christians. The first lady said, "I'm a Baptist, and here's my Bible to prove it." The second lady said, "I'm a Catholic, and here's my rosary to prove it." The third lady began rambling through this large pocketbook she had with her. Saint Peter asked her what she was doing. She said, "I'm a Methodist and there's a casserole in here someplace."

I have thought about that story since then. It is a good story. It is very important to study the Bible and live a life of prayer. It is also vitally important to live a life of service. Like the lady with the casserole, all of us can find some little thing we can do. We can find a way to serve. This will be our gift to Christ in the year ahead.

Give him the best thing that you have.

Then, move on to one thing more:

III

Let your life take a new direction.

If Christ is the object of your devotion and if you give to him the best you have, then your life will take a new direction.

We come now to a verse in this story that I love. We read these words: "And being warned in a dream not to return to Herod, they departed to their own country by another way." This means they did not go back to Jerusalem, through Herod's town. They avoided him and his suspicion. Maybe it also means they lived another way.

Maybe that could happen to us as we begin to move away from Christmas into the new year. Maybe we could return by another way.

Perhaps, this is the real test of Christmas, whether or not we have found something which cannot be lost, something that will carry us into the future by another way, on some new and different roads to a new place in our living. Perhaps, we can keep something of Christmas alive in us that will lead us into another way.

Long ago, Henry Van Dyke wrote these words we still remember today:

> *Are you willing to forget what you have done for other people, and remember what other people have done for you; to ignore what the world owes you, and think what you owe the world; to put your rights in the background, and your duties in the foreground; to own that probably the only good reason for your existence is not what you are going to get out of life, but what you are going to give life; to close your book of complaints against the management of the universe, and look around you for a place where you can sow a few seeds of happiness; are you willing to do these things even for a day? Then you can keep Christmas.*[2]

You can keep Christmas and you can take a new direction. You can carry with you into this new year the greatest blessings of this season.

Its love can live in our lives, and we can share it.

Its hope can hold us up, and give us patience.

Its joy can fill our hearts, and overflow into all our relationships.

Its peace can soothe our worried brows, and keep us calm within.

Its light can brighten our paths, and help us find our way.

A man watched his son playing on the floor. The boy seemed a little restless, so the man found a picture of the world in a magazine and cut it up into small pieces. He placed the pieces on the floor, and told the boy to see if he could put the world back together again, the way you would with a puzzle. He watched as the child got some tape and began to work. Then, the man read his paper for a while. But soon, the boy came to him with the world all taped back together. The man looked at it and then at his son and said, "How did you do this so quickly?" The boy replied, "It was really easy. There was a picture of Jesus on the other side of the page. I just put that picture together right and it made the whole world right."

If you will get this picture right in your thinking, it will make your life right, and as more and more of us do this, it makes the world right.

We take this with us away from Christmas as we return by another way. It is the way of devotion.

In the darkness of suspicion, may the light of devotion shine on you.

And remember, all the lights of Bethlehem still shine on.

---

1. James C. Cantrell, III, "Left Behind On Purpose," Chapel Notes, St. James United Methodist Church, Atlanta, Georgia, December 31, 1995.

2. Charles L. Allen and Charles L. Wallis, *Christmas* (Old Tappan, New Jersey: Fleming H. Revell Company, 1957), p, 42.

Epiphany Of Our Lord
Candlelighting and Prayer

Lighting Of The Christ Candle

Scripture Reading — Isaiah 53:1-9

*Who has believed what we have heard? And to whom
has the arm of the Lord been revealed? For he grew
up before him like a young plant, and like a root out of
dry ground; he had no form or majesty that we should
look at him, nothing in his appearance that we should
desire him. He was despised and rejected by others; a
man of suffering and acquainted with infirmity; and
as one from whom others hide their faces he was
despised, and we held him of no account.*

*Surely he has borne our infirmities and carried
our diseases; yet we accounted him stricken, struck
down by God, and afflicted. But he was wounded for
our transgressions, crushed for our iniquities; upon
him was the punishment that made us whole, and by
his bruises we are healed. All we like sheep have gone
astray; we have all turned to our own way, and the
Lord has laid on him the iniquity of us all. He was
oppressed and he was afflicted, yet he did not open his
mouth; like a lamb that is led to the slaughter, and like
a sheep that before its shearers is silent, so he did not
open his mouth. By a perversion of justice he was taken
away. Who could have imagined his future? For he
was cut off from the land of the living, stricken for the
transgression of my people. They made his grave with
the wicked and his tomb with the rich, although he had
done no violence, and there was no deceit in his mouth.*

Leader: This candle we light today helps us remember that Jesus
Christ is the light of the world, and to him we give our
devotion.

People: **Let this light of devotion shine through us. Thanks
be to God.**

81

Prayer

Our Father, who has graced the earth with the gift of thy Son and our Savior, Jesus Christ, and who has stooped low to deliver him to us, we gather today to worship thee, to thank thee, to praise thee for this most precious gift. Accept our worship, O God, as we thank thee for all good gifts, for thy gracious goodness we see at work in our lives in so many ways.

Most of all, Father, we thank thee for the gift of Christmas, for the Savior, his charming life, his atoning work, his healing touch, his forgiving ways, his uplifting hands, his redeeming friendship, his precious death, and his glorious resurrection.

As we thank thee for him, enable us to do something other than just admire him. Help us instead to accept him, to follow his example, to serve him, share him, and imitate him. Put us to work in his kingdom and in thy vineyard, if we have not yet taken up that work. If we have, then continue to use us and help us to imagine great things we might do for thee.

Make our faith strong, and enable us to face all that life brings our way. Help us stand in the face of danger, sickness, sorrow, fear, temptation, and doubt.

Forgive us when we fail thee, which is often. Make us anew in the image of thy Son.

Bless the sick of our church family and community. Be with those who may be in sorrow, out of work, alone, and those who feel helpless. Help them all, merciful Father.

Continue to bless the work and witness of this church. Bless the children and youth of our church family. Bless all the ministries we carry on, and all the people who are served by them.

Lead us, O God, into the year that is ahead of us. May it be a year of good work for thy kingdom, and may we build that kingdom in the lives of both people near us and around the world. And we pray in Jesus' name. Amen.

The People Of The Light, #7

Object: a crown Chrismon to put on the Chrismon tree

Boys and girls, today we will be thinking about the visit of the Wise Men, the three kings who came to see Jesus after he was born. Their visit is called the Day of Epiphany. It is observed twelve days after Christmas.

We are told in the Bible that they came looking for Jesus, having followed the light of a star for a long way. When they got to Jerusalem it was a big city and there were lots of lights everywhere. They lost sight of the star, but then they found out Jesus was supposed to be born in Bethlehem, so they went out there to find him. They followed the light of the star until it came to the place where he was. Then they went in to see him, and they presented their expensive gifts to him. They gave him gold, perfume, and spices.

So, the Chrismon we look at today is the crown. This reminds us of how the kings came to kneel down before Jesus and worship him. This crown reminds us of something else. Jesus was born to be a king. The kings bowed down before the King of kings.

What does a king do? A king rules, doesn't he? So, if we say Jesus is our king, then that means we are to let him rule our lives. We will live the way he wants us to live. We will obey him, and follow him. We will worship him, bow down before him, and give to him the best that we have.

Then, we will also try to make his kingdom real in the world around us. We will be witnesses for his kingdom. We will be servants for him.

All of us can be the people of the light in the way we live, the things we do, and the one we live for, and that is God's Son, Jesus Christ, who is the light of the world.